Auroville Reflected

Bindu Mohanty

2018

Acknowledgements

All texts are the copyright of the Sri Aurobindo Ashram Trust, Pondicherry, with the exception of the texts from Mother's Agenda.

Auroville Reflected
Copyright : Prisma, Auroville
Author : Bindu Mohanty

First edition 2013

ISBN 978-93-95460-55-2 (Paperpack)
ISBN 978-93-95460-50-7 (ebook)

BISAC Code:
HIS048000, HISTORY / Asia / Southeast Asia
LCO010000, LITERARY COLLECTIONS / Essays
REF000000, REFERENCE / General
LCO022030, LITERARY COLLECTIONS / Subjects & Themes / Places *

Thema Subject Category:
QDHC2, . oga (as a philosophy)
1FKA-IN-L, Southern India
1FKA-IN-LG, Puducherry
JHMC, Social and cultural anthropology

Cataloging-in-Publication Data for this title is available from the Library of Congress.

Published by:
PRISMA, an imprint of Digital Media Initiatives
PRISMA, Aurelec / Prayogshala,
Auroville 605101, Tamil Nadu, India
www.prisma.haus

With gratitude

to all those who have

helped to

build Auroville

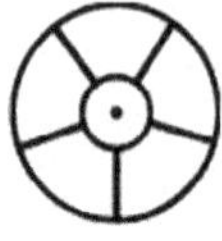

Auroville Charter

Auroville belongs to nobody in particular. Auroville belongs to humanity as a whole. But to live in Auroville one must be the willing servitor of the divine consciousness.

Auroville will be the place of an unending education, of constant progress, and a youth that never ages.

Auroville wants to be the bridge between the past and the future. Taking advantage of all discoveries from without and from within, Auroville will boldly spring towards future realizations.

Auroville will be a site of material and spiritual researches for a living embodiment of an actual human unity.

February 28, 1968

The Banyan Tree at the centre of Auroville in 1968

Foreword

The Evolutionary Context of Auroville

We can only know Auroville to the extent that we are in contact with the divine being in our own depths. That is why there is no use in "explaining" Auroville, for deep down you know it; only, the knowledge may be veiled. But that is your problem, to be worked out in your own way, your own yoga.
Ruud Lohmann (1939 – 1986) An Aurovilian

As an enormous banyan tree sleeps in the tiniest of seeds, so the ideal of Auroville is embedded in the evolution of life. Every child is born with it, every spiritual tradition alludes to it, and the perennial wisdom of humanity seeks it. The ideal of Auroville is not private, it is not sectarian, it belongs to everyone; it is universal. The town plan for Auroville is in the form of our galaxy. Auroville is a living symbol of our cosmic reality.

The seed for Auroville is the primal impulse of evolution: an inexorable urge toward expression through nature. Such a cosmology goes back 13.7 billion years, as science now tracks it; but for the purpose of this exploration, we can merely glance at the dawn of the twentieth century when certain historical changes became evident.

◄ *The Banyan Tree after 50 years*

In 1893, Swami Vivekananda has just awed the first Parliament of World Religions with a universal message for humanity. The industrial boom proposes to guarantee material prosperity for all. Science expects to have the solutions for disease and for practically everything else. Optimism is rising against the old tide of poverty, hunger, sickness, ignorance, and war.

Early in the twentieth century, two unique individuals furthered humanity's impulse for evolution, which eventually led to the founding of Auroville as the "city the earth needs": Aurobindo Ghose, equipped with a Cambridge education, just returned to his native India determined to free his homeland from the tyranny of the British Empire; Mirra Alfassa, an artist and intellectual, used her spiritual gifts to reach beyond her French culture. To groups in Europe, she communicated a vision of the future based upon human unity and the emergence of a new race.

Aurobindo Ghose then became "the most dangerous man in India" for the British. Jailed by the Crown, he had profound spiritual experiences in prison. Upon release, he left British India for the French territory of Pondicherry. In this quiet port, he realized his political activity had already made the liberation of India inevitable, while a far more daunting mission compelled his attention. He writes: "The principal object of my yoga is to remove absolutely and entirely every possible source of error and ineffectiveness . . . in order that the work of changing the world. . . may be entirely victorious and irresistible."[1]

Mirra Alfassa first visited Pondicherry with her husband who through some fortuitous circumstances received an appointment with Aurobindo Ghose. She recognized Aurobindo as a presence she had already seen in her visions. "We were standing side by side gazing out through the open window, and then together, at exactly the same moment, we felt, 'now the realization will be accomplished' . . . From that moment on there was nothing to say—no words,

---

1   Sri Aurobindo Birth Centenary Library. Vol. 26: 423-424.

nothing. We knew".[2] What had been a visionary experience now became an existential fact.

These two spiritual masters now began to bring the ideal into a concrete plan. Mirra Alfassa would later declare: "Auroville wants to be the first realization of human unity. . ."[3] But first, Aurobindo Ghose would become Sri Aurobindo as he reluctantly allowed a non-traditional ashram to form around him. He entrusted its organization to Mirra Alfassa, and confirmed the recognition of her spiritual status as "the Mother." In accord with the Vedic tradition, the Mother embodies the powers of the universal mother: strength (Mahakali), beauty (Mahalakshmi), wisdom (Mahaheswari), and perfection in work (Mahasaraswati). The Mother took charge of the Ashram and Sri Aurobindo secluded himself to write books and "bring down" the realization of the ideal while answering the enormous volume of correspondence from his disciples.

The optimism of that new century rapidly dissipated as war quickly overshadowed Europe. The havoc of two world wars and then a cold war with the threat of nuclear annihilation became the bitter legacy of the twentieth century. Science and capitalism profited, but the ideal of human unity faded as materialism and consumerism become the gods. Powered mostly by greed in its many guises, the first half of the twentieth century achieves technological breakthroughs without corresponding social and spiritual progress. At mid-century, Sri Aurobindo passed away and the "work" continued through the Mother.

In the early sixties, the Cuban missile crisis brought the United States and Russia to the brink of nuclear war. The Mother acted directly with a plan for an "international centre" to "give some concrete expression to the effort of transformation without violence." A positive response came from both Kennedy

---

2   Mother's Agenda. Vol. 2: 405-6.
3   Collected Works of the Mother. Vol. 13, 1978: 221.

and Khrushchev.[4] Prime Minister Nehru had summoned the American and Russian ambassadors to a meeting about the plan. Then Kennedy was assassinated and Khrushchev fell from power. Ultimately, it was UNESCO that actively endorsed Auroville (and continues to do so). M.S Adiseshiah Deputy Director-General of UNESCO, spoke at the inauguration of Auroville on February 28, 1968: "We have tried in UNESCO . . . we have tried every way, and we have failed. And so now we turn to Auroville, and to its foundation which [is] human unity . . . a hope for all of us, and particularly for our children".[5]

The inauguration of Auroville in 1968 caught the imagination of many around the world. Almost five thousand people thronged to the inaugural ceremony held in an earthen amphitheatre on a dusty plateau—barren, except for a lone banyan tree designated as the centre of the city-to-be. To symbolize the ideal of human unity, a marble-clad urn in the shape of a lotus bud had been built in this amphitheatre to receive the handfuls of earth brought from the countries of the world and the states of India. As two young representatives from each country placed their earth in the urn, All India Radio broadcast live to the world the Charter of Auroville read by the Mother from her room in Pondicherry.

A few pioneers moved onto this dusty plateau to build the city dedicated to human unity. For anything to take root in this unlikely place, a massive effort would be needed to restore this bit of earth. Fifty years later, after an estimated two million trees had been planted and erosion control measures were in place, the outer transformation became evident for anyone to see.

What is not evident for all to see, is what cannot be seen and what many have not yet even understood. This is where Bindu Mohanty's precise presentation becomes so essential and valuable. Not everyone realizes that the actual meaning

---

4   Mother's Agenda. Vol. 5: 28-9.
5   Sullivan, W. M. The Dawning of Auroville, 1992: 23.

and foundation of Auroville is germinated in the work of Sri Aurobindo and the Mother. Not to have some grip on this reality leads to missing the whole point of "why Auroville?". A concise and comprehensible access to that extensive yogic/ philosophical panorama is provided through her research and experience. Bindu's contribution is required reading for those who have not already had the good fortune of a background in what Sri Aurobindo and the Mother have given for the evolution of the human species. The core understanding of Sri Aurobindo's "planes and parts of the being", for example, opens up both the method and the universality of Integral Yoga. Mother's revelation of that in her own body, the consciousness of the cells, and her vision of grounding that in "matter", in a "city" of transformed beings living in human unity, is made clear. What is actually happening in Auroville's "laboratory of evolution" in contrast to the vision and the Dream, is also laid out in deft strokes to engage the readers who, like all of us, are part of this unique adventure.

B (William Sullivan)
12/12/2017

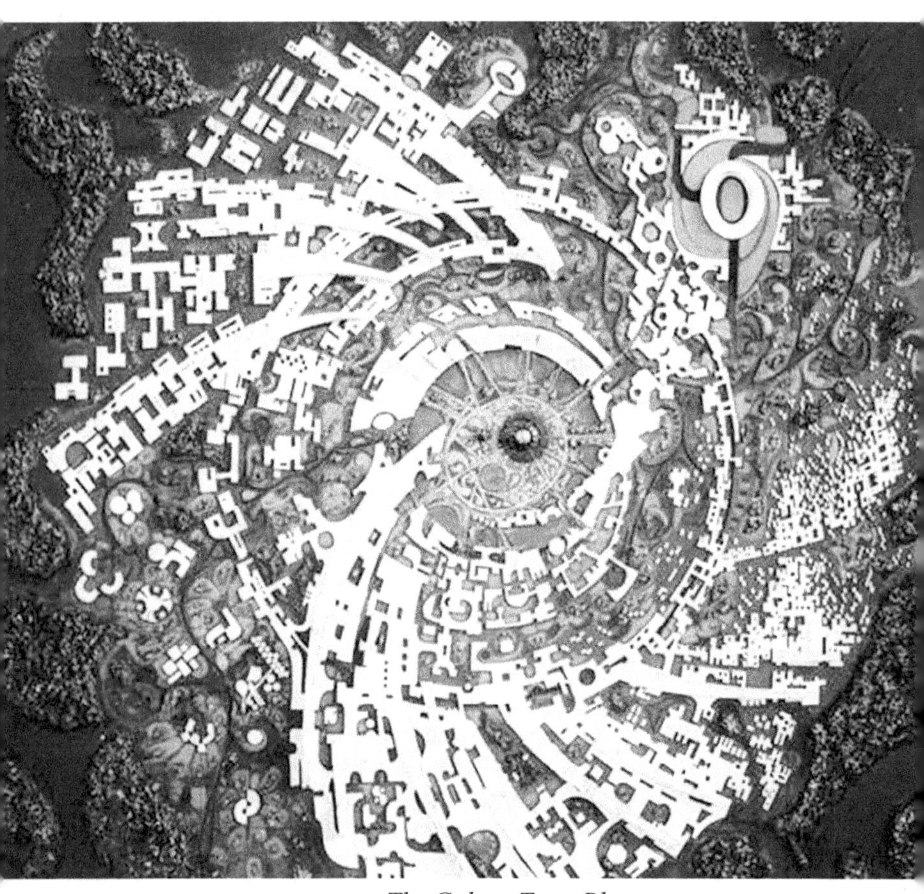

The Galaxy Town Plan

A Glimpse of Auroville

On 28 February 1968, young representatives of 124 nations from around the world, and all the states of India, placed a handful of earth in a lotus-shaped urn, thereby symbolically founding Auroville as a city of human unity. People with goodwill from all over the world were invited to join Auroville. Encouraged since its inception by UNESCO and with support from Government of India, Auroville has over two thousand eight hundred members from more than fifty countries. About 43% of its population is from India. Thousands of visitors, students, and guests also visit Auroville each year. Thirteen villages in the Indian state of Tamil Nadu are in the immediate bioregion of Auroville. This population of approximately 40,000 people, directly or indirectly, participate in the Auroville experiment.

In the last fifty years, Auroville has created a basic infrastructure with accommodation for its residents in over 100 settlements. Basic services for food, electricity and water supply, communication, waste management, education, health care, economic transactions, and town planning have been established. Auroville has also made commendable efforts towards promoting environmental regeneration, renewable energy and appropriate building technology, ecological agriculture, health care, educational research, handicrafts and small-scale industries, and rural development.

Auroville is a city-in-the-making spread over twenty square kilometres of a rural area. Its settlements are interspersed with village and private lands. Once a barren, deserted plateau, the site of Auroville has now been transformed into a livable environment after the planting of over two million trees. After five decades since its inception, Auroville is a small vibrant town that bustles with multifarious activities. Auroville actively engages in experiments of innovative forms of economic sharing, healing therapies, education and governance. With its intermingling of cultures and unbridled idealism, Auroville inspires artistic, cultural and athletic expressions in all its forms. A range of quality, hand-crafted products testify to Auroville's creativity and entrepreneurship.

An egalitarian society, the immovable assets of Auroville, though largely built through personal resources, donations and grants, are collectively held by the community of Auroville and accountable to the Auroville Foundation. There are networks of friends of Auroville everywhere, including Auroville International offices in many countries of the world.

Auroville is a dream—its evolutionary ideal of an actual human unity in diversity touches the hearts of many all over the world. Auroville embodies the deepest aspiration of humankind for a life that is imbued with meaning and conscious reflection.

A Crucible for Integral Yoga

People should know that coming to Auroville means an almost superhuman effort for progress.

The Mother

While Auroville welcomes all people who are drawn to the ideal of human unity, the deeper significance of Auroville can only be understood in the context of the spiritual path of Integral Yoga of Sri Aurobindo. Integral Yoga formulates a scientific and spiritual vision of evolution that evokes a complete transformation of the world and the birth of a new, spiritualized race. The scope and uniqueness of Sri Aurobindo's work comes from his unusual background and experiences. He received an entirely Western education without any contact with Indian languages or culture. A brilliant scholar in Greek and Latin, Sri Aurobindo was also well versed in French, German, and Italian. When he graduated from Cambridge, he was steeped in European culture. Upon returning to India at the age of twenty-one, he decided to learn Sanskrit and several modern Indian languages to assimilate the spirit of Indian culture and civilization. Sri Aurobindo became a synthesis of Indian and Western traditions, appealing to people from both the East and the West.

Sri Aurobindo's vision of life, detailed in over thirty volumes of the centenary edition of his works, traces the evolution of the human species through anthropology, sociology, politics, psychology, culture and religion. Most of his major works, namely *The Life Divine, The Synthesis of Yoga, Essays on the Gita, The Secret of the Veda, The Ideal of Human Unity* and *The Human Cycle* were written simultaneously between 1914-1920 and published in serialized form in a contemporaneous monthly philosophical review *The Arya*. The genius of Sri Aurobindo lies in the fact that he successfully reworks esoteric Indian spiritual thought in terms accessible to the modern, scientific thinker. In a tribute to him, noted transpersonal thinker Ken Wilber states:

> ***Aurobindo's genius was not merely that he captured the profundity of India's extraordinary spiritual heritage. He was the first great philosopher-sage to deeply grasp the nature and meaning of the modern idea of evolution. And thus, in Aurobindo, we have the first grand statement of an evolutionary spirituality that is an integration of the best of ancient wisdom and the brightest of modern knowledge ... nobody combined both philosophical brilliance and a profoundly enlightened consciousness the way Aurobindo did. His enlightenment informed his philosophy; his philosophy gave substance to his enlightenment; and that combination has been rarely equaled, in this or any time.***[6]

Parallels exist between the writings of Sri Aurobindo and other modern philosophers such as Hegel, Bergson, Teilhard de Chardin and Jean Gebser. Sri Aurobindo has also directly and indirectly influenced the disciplines of developmental

---

6   Wilber, Ken. A Greater Psychology - An Introduction to the Psychological Thought of Sri Aurobindo. 2000: Foreword, vii.

and transpersonal psychology. What perhaps differentiates Sri Aurobindo from these thinkers, however, is that he did not see himself as a philosopher, but made the "truth-claim" that his writing was derived directly from his spiritual experience, and he always sought to find a practical application of his knowledge. As Satprem, a French author, writes, "Sri Aurobindo said that the only utility of books and philosophies was not truly to enlighten the mind but to bring it to silence so that, calmed, it could pass to the experience and receive the direct inspiration."[7] After 1920, apart from his magnum opus, the epic *Savitri*, Sri Aurobindo's writing mainly finds expression through thousands of letters individually addressed to his disciples guiding them in their practice of Integral Yoga.

While many contemporary scholars, particularly from the West, overlook the contribution of The Mother in the development of Sri Aurobindo's yoga, Sri Aurobindo himself acknowledged her as his spiritual equal and collaborator. She was the moving force behind the Sri Aurobindo Ashram, founded in Pondicherry in 1926. Much later, in 1969, she described her role thus:

> ***The task of giving a concrete form to Sri Aurobindo's vision was entrusted to the Mother. The creation of a new world, a new humanity, a new society expressing and embodying the new consciousness is the work she has undertaken. … The Ashram founded and built by the Mother was the first step towards the accomplishment of this goal. The project of Auroville is the next step, more exterior, which seeks to widen the base of this attempt to establish harmony between soul and body, spirit and nature, heaven and earth, in the collective life of mankind.[8]***

---

7   Satprem. Sri Aurobindo or the Adventure of Consciousness. 1968: 293.

8   The Mother on Auroville, All India Press, 1977: 15.

It must not be forgotten that the "new world" Sri Aurobindo and the Mother envisioned is not based on the creation of a new religion or a new sect. They worked to transform the world for the next stage in the evolution of humankind by establishing a higher consciousness that they termed the Supermind. Their scope and vision is for all humanity, and the Sri Aurobindo Ashram and Auroville are "experiments" in collective living that can perhaps help humankind in its evolutionary journey. The ideal of Auroville is not just for Auroville, but for each individual and for the earth.

The Epistemology of Indian Spiritual Traditions

As Sri Aurobindo places himself in the millennia-old Vedic spiritual tradition of India, it is necessary to distinguish the epistemology of Indian philosophy from that of the West. To begin with, strictly speaking, there is no Indian equivalent for the word "philosophy", which literally means "love of wisdom". The corresponding word in Sanskrit for metaphysical or spiritual knowledge is *darshana*, which connotes "revealed wisdom". The Vedas, which form the fount of almost all Indian spiritual traditions, are referred to as *shruti* literature or knowledge that is revealed. Indian sages and mystics believe that beyond the sensory world there is a transcendental reality that can be grasped only by direct experience and not by the rationality of the intellect. So, unlike Western metaphysics, which is mostly based on the dialectic logic of the intellect, Indian metaphysics, especially in the Vedantic age, is based on spiritual experience which Sri Aurobindo refers to as "the logic of the Infinite".[9] The belief in intuitive knowledge, gained by direct experience and unmediated by social and cultural constructs, is accepted in all Indian spiritual traditions. Mystics claim that knowledge of a transcendental reality can be known and verified by following a requisite spiritual discipline.

---

9   Life Divine. 1972: 329.

While the transpersonal movement in the West acknowledges a transcendent or supra-rational dimension to human knowledge, the claims made by Indian or Eastern mystics have led to epistemological problems for social scientists, especially as the nature of the transcendent reality is described differently in different traditions. As Peter Heehs points out in his book *Indian Religions*: "Are mystics right in thinking that what they feel themselves to be in contact with is (the) reality? Do their private experiences put them in a position to make claims about the nature of life and the world? If these truth-claims disagree with one another, are some or all of them refuted? Is there one Truth or many truths, or is 'truth' a human construction determined by social and political forces…?"[10] The tenets of Integral Yoga, especially those that deal with the nature of transcendental reality, can either be accepted on faith or considered as truth-claims. It needs to be pointed out, however, that throughout his voluminous writings Sri Aurobindo expresses a worldview that is comprehensive, consistent, and a convincing explanation of manifest reality. In this regard, Sri Aurobindo is unparalleled by any philosopher in the East or West.

The Metaphysics of Sri Aurobindo's Vision

Sri Aurobindo's teaching starts with the ancient Vedantic premise of the One Self, or Brahman, as the ultimate creator: omnipotent, omniscient, and omnipresent; who is all that is created and is yet beyond creation. This One Self expresses itself in creation through myriads of forms and, through the process of evolution, these multitudes of forms seek to recover their essential unity (an unity-in-differentiation) in the One Self. As Sri Aurobindo puts it, "All evolution is the progressive self-

---

10 Heehs, Peter. Indian Religions: The Spiritual Traditions of South Asia. 2002: 20.

revelation of the One to himself."[11]

Essentially, the One Self, or *Brahman*, is described in the Vedanta as *Sachchidananda*, having the triune attributes of *Sat* (absolute existence), *Chit-Tapas* (absolute consciousness and force), and *Ananda* (absolute bliss). Both Eastern and Western philosophers recognize that all of creation essentially consists of an exterior form that is animated by an inner force or consciousness. Indian philosophy holds that it is the attribute of *Sat* that determines the exterior form, while that of *Chit-Tapas* determines the force or consciousness contained within the form. Everything in this creation exhibits these two essential attributes of *Sat* and *Chit-Tapas* as form and consciousness-force.

According to ancient Indian scriptures and re-affirmed by Sri Aurobindo, creation is seen as a divine "lila" or play, the raison d'être of which is Ananda or bliss: "From Ananda," says the Upanishad, "all existences are born, by Ananda they remain in being and increase, to Ananda they depart."[12]

Like Hegel before him, Sri Aurobindo posits that in order for evolution to take place, there must have been an involution of the Self in matter: "Evolution of Life in matter supposes a previous involution of it there, unless we suppose it to be a new creation magically and unaccountably introduced into Nature." Elsewhere, Sri Aurobindo describes this process of involution and evolution as:

> ***This One Being and Consciousness [Sachchidananda] is involved here in Matter. Evolution is the method by which it liberates itself; consciousness appears in what seems to be inconscient, and once having appeared is self-impelled to grow higher and higher and at the***

---

11 Essays Divine and Human: 1972: 219.
12 Quoted in Life Divine: 101.

same time to enlarge and develop towards a greater and greater perfection. Life is the first step of this release of consciousness; mind is the second; but the evolution does not finish with mind, it awaits a release into something greater, a consciousness which is spiritual and supramental. The next step of the evolution must be towards the development of Supermind and Spirit as the dominant power in the conscious being. For only then will the involved Divinity in things release itself entirely and it become possible for life to manifest perfection.[13]

In short, matter, life (also referred to as "the vital" by Sri Aurobindo) and mind form the basis of our earthly existence. This much is verified by science and accepted by all modern evolutionary theorists. Sri Aurobindo, however, further postulates that as mind is still limited in its power and knowledge and is a divisive consciousness, there is a fourth principle, the principle of Supermind, endowed with divine attributes of infinite power and integral knowledge, which, through the process of evolution, will one day be fully manifested on Earth.

In *The Life Divine*, which is an exposition of his metaphysical vision of evolution, Sri Aurobindo explains at length that if *Brahman*, the One Self, is involved in matter, then its attributes of *Sat*, *Chit* and *Ananda* are involved or hidden in matter. Each higher level of evolution progressively reveals the nature of Brahman; that is to say, each evolutionary level – from matter to plants to animals to human beings and ultimately to supramental beings – expresses more and more the qualities of *Sat* and *Chit* and *Ananda*. As one proceeds upwards on the evolutionary scale from matter to life to mind, one observes that the material density or rigidity of the form decreases and the consciousness expressed by the form increases. At every significant evolutionary stage, new

---

13   Quoted in Life Divine: 185.

forms with an increasingly complex expression of consciousness are produced. In other words, out of hard, inanimate rocks, plants capable of showing response arose; out of plants, animals capable of instinctive reaction arose; and out of animals, human beings with a rational will arose. The third principle of *Ananda* or Bliss manifests itself, according to Sri Aurobindo, as a secret desire towards recovering the essential unity of *Sachchidananda.* Therefore in the evolutionary scale, *Ananda* expresses itself as the force of attraction in matter, hunger in the physical-vital domain, desire in the vital, and love in the mental domain of human beings.[14] As "evolution is not finished ... nor the reasoning animal the supreme figure of Nature,"[15] it follows out of logical necessity that at the supramental level, a stage of consciousness much higher than the mind, a new form or the supramental species will be manifested on Earth. Sri Aurobindo describes this superman or the supramental race as possessing all the divine qualities of *Sachchidananda,* namely immortality, absolute consciousness, omnipotence and unity. Says Sri Aurobindo:

As man emerged out of the animal, so out of man, the superman emerges.[16]

The Influence of Typal Planes

Hegel believed that the Spirit (or Self) seeks to become infinite by its struggle to overcome the finite. Sri Aurobindo, however, holds that the Self or *Sachchidananda,* never loses its infinity or omnipotence. This hypothesis lends itself to some important philosophical ramifications. To begin with, the Self, being infinite and omnipotent, does not have any limitations other than what it chooses to impose upon itself. It is free to express itself not

---

14   Sri Aurobindo on Himself: 1972: 95.
15   Life Divine: 194-197.
16   Essays Divine and Human: 443.

just through the process of evolution but in various other ways. Building on this premise, Sri Aurobindo posits that during the process of involution seven subtle, "typal" worlds were created that expressed an essential quality of the Self or *Sachchidananda:* "All that manifested from the Eternal has already been arranged in worlds or planes of its own nature, planes of subtle Matter, planes of Life, planes of Mind, planes of Supermind, planes of the triune luminous Infinite [i.e. the three planes of *Sat, Chit* and *Ananda,* which together comprise *Sachchidananda*]. But these worlds or planes are not evolutionary but typal. A typal world is one in which some ruling principle manifests itself in its free and full capacity."[17]

To the modern evolutionary theorist, belief in such intangible and occult worlds would be inadmissible given the lack of objective proof. But Sri Aurobindo, citing his own spiritual experience as evidence and decidedly dismissing the limitations of sensorial-experience, states: "Not having bound ourselves down, like so much of modern thought, to the dogma that … the analysis of physical experience by the reason alone [is] verifiable … and anything beyond this an error, self-delusion and hallucination, we are free to accept this evidence and to admit the reality of these planes."[18] It could be mentioned in passing that Sri Aurobindo's description of the typal planes is in keeping with that of the ancient Vedantic seers who spoke of the "sevenfold chord of Existence", or the existence of seven occult planes beyond the material world.

For Sri Aurobindo, the existence of typal planes is fundamental to understanding the complex process of evolution: "The development of Life, Mind and Spirit in the physical being presupposes their existence [that of typal planes]; for these powers are developed here by two co-operating forces,

---

17 Essays Divine and Human: 236.
18 Life Divine: 787-88.

an upward-tending force from below, an upward-drawing and downward-pressing force from above."[19] He explains that without the influence of typal planes from above, the Spirit could have remained forever imprisoned in Matter, for there is no justification as to why Matter, on its own accord, should evolve to liberate the Spirit involved within it. Conception is a useful analogy to understand these ascending and descending forces of the evolutionary process. Conception takes place only when the womb is ready for impregnation. At each level of evolution, when the Earth (the material womb) was ready to take an evolutionary leap upwards, there was a descent of the corresponding typal plane onto Earth. That is to say, the principle of the Mind descended onto Earth from the Mental Plane, long before human beings possessing the instrument of mind were born. Similarly, the spiritual consciousness of the Supermind is believed to now be active on Earth, having descended from the supramental plane from above. As Sri Aurobindo explains:

A secret continuous action of the higher powers and principles from their own planes upon terrestrial being and nature ... must have an effect and a significance. Its first effect has been the liberation of Life and Mind out of Matter; its last effect has been to assist the emergence of a spiritual consciousness.[20]

According to the Mother, the supramental manifestation upon earth took place in 1956, and in 300 years or more, depending upon the capacity of human beings for progress, the Earth will witness the birth of a new species, the supramental race.

Considering that it took at least 200,000 years from the emergence of Homo sapiens to the full flowering of powers

---

19   Life Divine: 790.
20   ibid.: 821.

of the mind as evidenced today, 300 years is a mere blink of an eye on the evolutionary timescale. For Sri Aurobindo and the Mother, the advent of a supramental age is a certitude. As the Mother, in a decisive message to the disciples in 1956 said, "The manifestation of the supramental upon earth is no more a promise but a living fact, a reality. It is at work here, and one day will come when the most blind, the most unconscious, even the most unwilling shall be obliged to recognize it."[21] It is to be noted, however, that both Sri Aurobindo and the Mother discouraged unnecessary speculation among the disciples about the effects that the supramental consciousness would have on the world, believing that this omnipotent divine power would work things out in its own way and at its own pace.

The Principle of Descent

The idea of a descent of a divine power from higher planes is not widely accepted in Western theology or spiritual metaphysics, though there are references to it in the writings of certain Greek philosophers, namely, Heraclitus, Plato, and Plotinus. Modern thinkers, such as Arthur Lovejoy and Ken Wilber, have also sought to elaborate on this philosophical tenet, but the concept of a "divine descent" is elaborated to its fullness only in the Hindu tradition. Sri Aurobindo's description of the various kinds of "descent" of the omnipotent Self includes and goes beyond Wilber's concept of descent or *"agape"* (the higher reaching down and embracing the lower).[22] In the Indian tradition, one important form of descent is the avatar, which "is a direct incarnation of the Divine in his manifestation to make the next higher step in evolution possible; for the topmost established level of evolution, though driven to develop by the inherent evolutionary impulse,

---

21   Collected Works of the Mother: Vol. 8: 145.
22   Wilber, Ken. Sex, Ecology, Spirituality: The Spirit of Evolution (SES). 1995: 338.

is unable to pierce the existing ceiling of progress."[23] While Sri Aurobindo and the Mother did not refer to themselves as avatars, they regarded themselves as evolutionary pathfinders who played a crucial role in bringing down the principle of the Supermind or the supramental consciousness onto Earth.

At first glance, the idea that an individual can decisively help in the evolutionary process of the human species seems unwarranted. But psychologist Allan Combs, accepting the possibility that Sri Aurobindo and the Mother could well have broken new "evolutionary ground for the entire human species", points out:

Two Western scientific theorists ... have advanced carefully considered hypotheses which support the idea that a few persons, or even a single individual, could conceivably alter the entire future of the human potential. These hypotheses are of such enormous potential importance to the whole topic of evolution."[24]

The Yoga of the Mother

Sri Aurobindo and the Mother regarded themselves as expressing a single consciousness embodied in two different bodies. After Sri Aurobindo passed away in 1950, the Mother continued the work of "making available ... transformative energies of the highest realms of the Divine available to human beings."[25] The Mother stated that even after Sri Aurobindo's physical demise, she was guided in an occult way by "the Sri Aurobindo whom I know and with whom I lived physically for thirty years, and who has not left me, not for a moment – for he is still with me, day and night, thinking through my

---

23 Vrekhem, Georges Van. Overman: The Intermediary Between The Human and the Supramental Being. 2001: 17.

24 Combs, Allan. The Radiance of Being: Complexity, Chaos and the Evolution of Consciousness. 1996: 149-50.

25 Combs, ibid.: 60.

brain, writing through my pen, speaking through my mouth and acting through my organizing power."[26]

Georges Van Vrekhem, a contemporary interpreter of Sri Aurobindo's and the Mother's work, writes that Sri Aurobindo consciously chose to leave his physical body in order to help in the spiritual transformation of life from an occult plane. On earth, after Sri Aurobindo's passing, the Mother continued the task of transforming matter and her own physical body from the point Sri Aurobindo had reached. Her first step was to realize that in order to build an immortal body, the consciousness of the cells of the body needs to be divinized. At a later stage she worked to transform the subconscient and the inconscient realms, which, in the context of Sri Aurobindo's cosmology, are regarded as the foundation of the plane of matter.

A singular achievement was the supramental manifestation in 1956 during which, as the Mother explained, the evolutionary and transformative principle of the Supermind descended onto the earth on a universal scale, thereby changing and hastening the process of earthly evolution. From 1956, the year of the supramental manifestation, until the time of her own passing in 1973, the Mother worked to form a prototype supramental body by changing the cellular consciousness of her own body cells. Many, notably Georges Van Vrekhem, hold that the Mother succeeded in this work, and that this prototype of an immortal and supramental body exists on an occult plane and will one day be physically manifested on earth. Her psychological and spiritual experiences during this period are recorded as transcripts of conversations and posthumously published by the Institute of Evolutionary Research in thirteen volumes as *The Mother's Agenda*.

---

26 Pandit, M.P. (ed.) Champaklal Speaks. 1975: 251.

Integral Yoga as a Conscious Process

While the evolutionary progress from the mind to the Supermind is an inevitable natural process and does not depend on the human will, human beings can consciously choose to participate in the process and hasten the birth of the new species. Sri Aurobindo explains:

The former steps in evolution, were taken by Nature without a conscious will in the plant and animal life; in man Nature becomes able to evolve by a conscious will in the instrument.[27]

It is not so easy however for individuals to exercise their conscious will, as human beings are a complex amalgam of different desires arising from different parts of their being. The fact that man is made up of various interrelated parts of being is accepted by almost all spiritual traditions of the world. Perennial philosophy refers to it as the "Great Nest of Being" and points out that the human being comprises "various levels of existence … ranging from matter to body to mind to soul to spirit."[28] Sri Aurobindo explains that in the course of evolution from matter to life to mind, the human being has acquired a physical body, a vital (emotional) body and a mental body. But, in Sri Aurobindo's classification, these three planes – the physical, the vital and the mental – merely represent the tip of the iceberg of an individual's consciousness. These three planes form the outer nature or the ego personality of the individual, which governs its waking consciousness.

Sri Aurobindo further classifies in detail almost a dozen planes of being that lie above, below and within this outer nature,

---

27   Sri Aurobindo on Himself. 95.
28   Wilber, Ken. Integral Psychology: Consciousness, Spirit, Psychology, Therapy. 2000: 5.

respectively termed the supraconscient, the subconscient and the subliminal. In Sri Aurobindo's vision, the micro-cosmos of the individual nature corresponds to and connects with the macro-cosmos of the typal worlds of the universe. Moreover, Sri Aurobindo holds that, both in the micro-cosmos and the macro-cosmos, each plane of being is governed by its own laws and its own unique consciousness. For instance, in the micro-cosmos, the physical body has a body consciousness that is prone to inertia and mechanical or habitual responses to stimuli. The part of the mind that Sri Aurobindo terms the physical mind is associated with the body consciousness.

Similarly ruling the emotional body of the human being is a vital consciousness and a vital mind that is driven by desires, reactions and impulses. Mind proper, or the mental consciousness, has the capability of self-reflection and rationalization. The human being is usually not able to differentiate between these three different minds arising from different planes for, as Sri Aurobindo says, "in our waking experience, they are all confused together." These different planes of being, both in the micro-cosmos and the macro-cosmos, tend to exert their laws or ways of working on the individual, who then has to be aware of these influences and consciously participate in the evolutionary process.

The supraconscient realm (the realm above the rational consciousness of the mind), according to Sri Aurobindo, consists of five hierarchical levels of consciousness that connect the ordinary mind of the individual to the universal Supermind. At each higher level of consciousness, the individual experiences manifest reality differently and in an increasingly more integral manner.

A unique feature of Sri Aurobindo's description of human psychology is the concept of an individualized soul or psychic being. This psychic being, an unalloyed part of the Divine, is the innermost centre in the human being, hidden from the surface consciousness by all the other planes of being that envelop it.

In keeping with other spiritual traditions, Sri Aurobindo accepts that the soul has a universal aspect that is one with all. But he also states that there is a soul individuality or psychic being, which evolves over lifetimes. This is one's true individual personality (as opposed to the ego personality) that one needs to express in order to manifest a divine life on earth.

> ***The soul is something of the Divine that descends into the evolution as a Divine Principle within it to support the evolution of the individual out of the Ignorance into the Light. It develops in the course of the evolution a psychic individual or soul individuality which grows from life to life, using the evolving mind, vital and body as its instruments. It is the soul that is immortal while the rest disintegrates; it passes from life to life carrying its experiences in essence and the continuity of the evolution of the individual.[29]***

While the presence of the psychic being is rarely felt in our ordinary consciousness, through a conscious spiritual discipline or through successive reincarnations the psychic being progressively manifests itself by bringing the outer nature under its direct control. This process of discovering the psychic being and allowing it to integrate and govern the different planes of one's being is termed by Sri Aurobindo the *psychic transformation*. An individual's conscious participation in the evolutionary process begins only with this first step of a *psychic transformation*.

Integral Transformation

To help individuals to consciously participate in the evolutionary process, Sri Aurobindo and the Mother formulated a conscious discipline, which is the basis of the Integral

---

29   Sri Aurobindo. Letters on Yoga: 1972: 347.

Yoga. The Sanskrit word "yoga" connotes union with the Divine. And, "Integral Yoga is so called because it aims at a harmonized totality of spiritual realization and experience. Its aim is integral experience of the divine reality. … Its method is an integral opening of the whole consciousness, mind, heart, life, will, body to that reality, to the divine existence, consciousness, beatitude, to its being and its integral transformation of the whole nature."[30]

Sri Aurobindo spells out three steps of progressive self-achievement that lead to the integral transformation. The first is the psychic transformation in which the individual acts from the guidance of the psychic being rather than the ego. The next step, often concurrent with the first, is to become aware of the universal self that is one in all. The third step is the supramental transformation by which the power of the Supermind acts on the individual and transforms him into a supramental being.

In India, for thousands of years, different spiritual traditions have advocated different spiritual disciplines leading to liberation from the determinisms of the world. Comparing his path to other disciplines, Sri Aurobindo states:

In the past, it [realization of the Spirit] has been attempted by a drawing away from the world and a disappearance into the height of the Self or Spirit. Sri Aurobindo teaches that a descent of the higher principle is possible which will not merely release the spiritual Self out of the world, but release it in the world … and make it possible for the human being to find himself dynamically as well as inwardly and grow out of his still animal humanity into a diviner race. The psychological discipline of Yoga can be used to that end by opening all the parts of the being to a conversion or transformation through the descent

---

30   Quoted in Wilber, SES: 97.

and working of the higher still concealed supramental principle.[31]

In short, Integral Yoga seeks not a renunciation of life and liberation from the world but a transformation of life and the world, not a rejection of the different egoistic parts of one's being but a transformation and integration of those parts into a divine nature.

"This, however," Sri Aurobindo warns, "cannot be done at once or in a short time or by any rapid or miraculous transformation. … For there are several ranges of consciousness between the ordinary human mind and the supramental truth-consciousness. … [that] have to be opened up and their power brought down into the mind, life and body."[32] To help in this laborious process of a spiritual transformation through yoga, Sri Aurobindo emphasizes the need for a constant aspiration for the Divine, for a total rejection of one's egoistic desires and a complete surrender to the divine supramental force. Surrender is an important aspect in Sri Aurobindo's yoga, for it is apparent that the individual with his limited consciousness cannot achieve the supramental consciousness on his own. It is only by the descent of the divine power from the supramental plane that the supramental transformation of the individual can be accomplished. Besides, in Sri Aurobindo's perception, the power of the individual is limited, while that of the Supermind is infinite. So, the easiest way for individuals to progress on the spiritual path and to transform themselves is to surrender to the working of the Supermind – the highest power of the Divine. Many followers of Sri Aurobindo regard the Mother as a personification of the divine force to whom they can make their surrender, and they refer to the Mother's force as the supramental force acting in the world.

At the same time, Sri Aurobindo's Integral Yoga, unlike

---

31 Sri Aurobindo on Himself: 96.
32 ibid.: 96-97.

any other spiritual discipline, gives immense freedom to individuals to pursue their inner self-development according to their nature. This tenet of Integral Yoga stems from the belief of the psychic being within each person representing a unique and true individuality that needs to be expressed in the world. The Mother once said that the best way to collaborate in the supramental transformation is "to realize one's being under no matter what form, by no matter what road … Each individual carries in himself a truth and it is with this truth that he must unite himself, it is this truth he must live; and in this way the road he follows to realize this truth becomes also the road which will bring him the nearest possible to the transformation."[33]As Integral Yoga seeks to bring about a spiritual transformation of life in the material conditions of the earth, utmost importance is given to one's dealing with the material world. This takes many forms: from seeking the perfection of the body through physical exercise, to taking care of the material things one uses, from engaging in regular physical work, to cultivating an appreciation for beauty and aesthetics, and leading a conscious life.

According to Sri Aurobindo and the Mother, matter, despite its inertia and unconsciousness, embodies the divine consciousness, and thus commands utmost respect. They taught that by engaging with the material world consciously, through one's work and activities, one can effect a change in matter. As the Mother explained:

Work, even manual work, is something indispensable for the inner discovery. If one does not work, if one does not put his consciousness into matter, the latter will never develop. … To establish order around oneself helps to bring order within oneself.[34]

---

33 Quoted in Satprem, AC: 353.
34 Mother's Agenda. Vol. 11, 1981: 248.

Similarly, the body, the material basis of existence, is regarded as an instrument of the Divine that has to be perfected through disciplined physical education so that it can embody a higher consciousness. A lifestyle that embraces a healthy diet, proper rest, exercise, balanced work and play, all become essential. The cultivation of beauty in one's physical surroundings stems from the fact that "in the physical world, of all things it is beauty that best expresses the Divine ... Beauty interprets, expresses, manifests the Eternal."[35]

A Collective Yoga

Integral Yoga does not stop at the individual realization, but seeks a transformation of earthly nature:

> ***For this transformation to succeed, all human beings – even all living beings as well as their material environment – must be transformed. Otherwise things will remain as they are: an individual experience cannot change terrestrial life. ... Not only an individual or a group of individuals, or even all individuals, but life ... has to be transformed.[36]***

Some surmise that each individual who takes up the yoga represents a certain universal psychological difficulty that needs to be transformed, and if the transformation is achieved in one individual, then that has an effect on the whole of humanity. Supporting such a belief, the evolutionary scientist Rupert Sheldrake postulates that "if one member of a biological species learns a new behavior, the morphogenic field for the species changes, even if very slightly. If the behavior is repeated long enough, its morphic resonance builds up and begins to affect

---

35 Collected Works of the Mother. Vol. 12: 234.
36 ibid. Vol. 15: 316.

the entire species."[37] A corollary to this belief is the fact that the transformation cannot be carried out by a single individual, for he/she represents only one particular type of personality. In order to achieve a complete transformation of human nature, all personality-types need to be represented in this collective yoga for humanity. Mother affirms, "By the very nature of things, it [the supramental transformation] is a collective ideal that calls for a collective effort so that it may be realized in the terms of an integral human perfection".[38]

For the individual practitioner of Integral Yoga, there comes a point at which one no longer does the yoga for oneself, but more and more for everybody. Calling his yoga "yoga for the earth-consciousness", Sri Aurobindo holds that an individual's spiritual endeavour is linked to the collective effort for progress:

Accepting life, he (the seeker of the Integral Yoga) has to bear not only his own burden, but a great part of the world's burden too along with it, as a continuation of his own sufficiently heavy load. Therefore his Yoga has much more the nature of a battle than others'; but this is not only an individual battle, it is a collective war waged over a considerable country. He has not only to conquer in himself the forces of egoistic falsehood and disorder, but to conquer them as representatives of the same adverse and inexhaustible forces in the world.[39]

This collective aspect of Integral Yoga needs to be differentiated from the type of community living sometimes sought by spiritual seekers. A collective yoga, or even a collective

---

37　Quoted in Russell, Peter. The Global Brain Awakens: Our Next Evolutionary Leap. 1995: 316.

38　Collected Works of the Mother. Vol. 13: 210.

39　Sri Aurobindo. The Synthesis of Yoga: 1972: 71.

effort for transformation, does not necessarily imply that the practitioners of Integral Yoga have to do things together in their outer, daily life. Visitors to Auroville are sometimes dismayed by the seeming lack of community in Auroville – that there are no shared spiritual practices and few community rituals or celebrations. Elaborating on the idea of true community, the Mother says, "One of the most common types of human collectivity [is] to group together … around a common ideal … but in an artificial way. In contrast to this … a true community can be based only on the inner realization of each one of its members."[40] The individual's inner growth expresses itself naturally through the collective.

Human Unity

Complementary to the idea of collective yoga, is Sri Aurobindo's ideal of an actual human unity. For Sri Aurobindo, the ideal of human unity stems from the fact that underlying all appearances, "there is a secret spirit, a divine reality [the One Self, or *Sachchidananda*], in which we are all one."[41] He says that if one were to start from this spiritual premise of unity, then there would be "free room for the realization of the highest human dreams, for the perfectibility of the race, a perfect society, a higher upward evolution of the human soul and human nature."[42] Sri Aurobindo holds that a mere intellectual belief in human unity is doomed to failure, for actual human unity can only be achieved by the progressive spiritual realization of the oneness of the whole universe. In his epic *Savitri*, he gives this key concept a lyrical and decisive expression: "To feel love and oneness is to live. And this the magic of our golden change".[43]

---

40 Mother's Agenda. Vol. 1: 107.
41 Sri Aurobino. The Human Cycle, 1972: 577.
42 ibid.: 586.
43 Sri Aurobindo. Savitri, 2007: 724.

The spiritual ideal of human unity does not mean a homogenization or outward uniformity, but rather a unity that celebrates the essential diversity of all creation. For Sri Aurobindo, each individual, in his psychic being, represents a unique aspect of the infinite diversity of the Divine, and Integral Yoga is a process by which individuals manifest the unique divine personality within them, and by doing so find their place in the ordered harmony of the supramental creation. An "actual human unity", the aim of Auroville as spelled out in its Charter, essentially implies a spiritual society where individuals manifest their psychic beings. Sri Aurobindo elaborates on his ideas of "a perfect society" thus:

A spiritualized society would treat in its sociology the individual, from the saint to the criminal, not as units of a social problem to be passed through some skillfully devised machinery and either flattened into the social mould or crushed out of it, but as souls suffering and entangled in a net and to be rescued, souls growing and to be encouraged to grow, souls grown and from whom help and power can be drawn by the lesser spirits who are not yet adult.[44]

Sri Aurobindo also believed that if this ideal of human unity was not taken up in one form or the other, then there could be disastrous consequences for the whole race. Reportedly communicating to the Mother from an occult plane, Sri Aurobindo said that the manifestation of Auroville would be "a practical means creating a human unity that would be strong enough to fight against war."[45]

---

44   Life Divine: 257.
45   Mother's Agenda. Vol. 7: 222.

The Inauguration of Auroville on 28 February 1968

Auroville as "A City the Earth Needs"

Auroville is intended to hasten the advent of the supramental reality upon earth.

The Mother

In innumerable ways, perhaps even unknown to its residents, Auroville is an experimental field for Sri Aurobindo's and the Mother's work towards a spiritual transformation of the world. Auroville, planned as a township for 50,000 people, can be seen as a step towards establishing a spiritualized society. While in some messages, especially the early ones, the Mother seems to indicate that having goodwill is a sufficient qualification to become an Aurovilian, from many other recorded conversations it is clear that she expected Aurovilians to "belong to the enlightened portion of humanity"[46] and to be open to the "discovery and practice of the divine consciousness that is seeking to manifest itself."[47] The Auroville Charter explicitly states that, "to live in Auroville, one must be the willing servitor of the divine consciousness."[48] During her lifetime, the Mother hand-picked who would be admitted from those who applied to join Auroville.

---

46 Collected Works of the Mother. Vol. 13: 216.
47 Mother's Agenda. Vol. 10: 354-55.
48 ibid. Vol. 9: 68.

Whether the residents of Auroville consciously practice the Integral Yoga or not, it is believed that each individual has a role to play in the collective transformation of humanity in accordance with Sri Aurobindo's teaching:

For a spiritual and supramental yoga, humanity should be variously represented. For the problem of transformation has to deal with all sorts of elements favourable and unfavourable. The same man indeed carries in him a mixture of these two things. If only sattwic (virtuous) and cultured men come for yoga, men without very much of the vital difficulty in them, then, because the difficulty of the vital element in terrestrial nature has not been faced and overcome, it might well be that the endeavour would fail.[49]

As Integral Yoga allows for a free self-development of the individual and the progressive manifestation of his unique psychic being, Aurovilians have utmost freedom in their spiritual practice and way of life. The point is not about individuals following any particular set of beliefs, but rather about how one lives and contributes both to the evolving community of Auroville and their own self-development. Of course, the freedom that Aurovilians enjoy does not mean that people can give free rein to any desire. The Mother reminds Aurovilians that "the only true freedom is the one obtained by union with the Divine. One can unite with the Divine only by mastering one's ego."[50]

Why a City?

Designated by the Mother "the city the Earth needs", Auroville can be seen as a micro-cosmic representation of

---

49   Sri Aurobindo. Letters on Yoga: 355.
50   The Mother on Auroville: 1977: 32.

humanity that would have a transformative effect on the macro-cosmos of the world. The Mother conceived it as "a centre of transformation, a small nucleus of men who are transforming themselves and setting an example for the world."[51] Even though the Mother categorically states that "as long as egoism and bad will exist in the world, a general transformation is impossible"[52], there are certain symbols inherent in its town plan that indicate ways in which Auroville can have an effect on the larger world.

To begin with, a city – as opposed to a village or community – is perhaps the smallest collective unit that contains all the activities that human beings usually engage in. If these activities are undertaken, not from the basis of personal desire, but in the spirit of yoga, then it is feasible that a spiritual transformation of human life can take place. Yet another symbol is in the fact that the Mother purposely situated Auroville in India, for as she stated, "India is the representation of all human difficulties on earth, and it is in India that there will be … the cure. And it is for that – it is FOR THAT that I had to create Auroville [emphasis in original]."[53] It is perhaps not a mere coincidence that Auroville was founded on an environmentally-degraded wasteland in an impoverished area of rural southern India. The land was so badly eroded that a District Forest Officer visiting the area in 1976 noted: "The entire area is exposed to wind and water erosion. If this is allowed to continue, then … the people will be forced to vacate the land in the not too distant future."[54] It is to the credit of pioneering Aurovilians that through massive environmental regeneration efforts today the rural bioregion of Auroville has recovered and thrives.

---

51 Collected Works of the Mother. Vol. 13: 225.
52 ibid. Vol. 13: 225.
53 Mother's Agenda. Vol. 9: 41-42.
54 Auroville: A city that cares for its bioregion. 1998: 3.

The Soul of the City: Matrimandir

The layout of the city of Auroville is symbolic. The town plan itself resembles a spiral galaxy, like that of our own. At the centre of the town plan is an oval-shaped area, designated by the Mother as an "area of peace." At the exact geographic centre, and pre-dating the founding of Auroville, is a banyan tree, sacred in Indian culture. Next to the tree is an amphitheatre constructed for the inauguration of Auroville in 1968, with a central urn which contains the soil from 124 countries that were represented during the inaugural ceremony. Next to the banyan and the amphitheatre, and in triangular orientation to them, is Matrimandir, a golden disc-clad globe containing an inner chamber for concentration, which the community spent thirty-seven years building as "the soul of Auroville."[55]

The Matrimandir is "the symbol of the Universal Mother according to Sri Aurobindo's teaching,"[56] but not as a temple or memorial. For Sri Aurobindo, the Universal Mother represents the supramental consciousness, or the conscious evolutionary divine power that seeks to help humanity move beyond its present limitations into the next step of its evolutionary adventure. The Matrimandir, said Mother, is "a symbol of the Divine's answer to man's aspiration for perfection."[57] For most Aurovilians, the Matrimandir is "the central cohesive force"[58] that unites this diverse community and the multi-faceted activities of the township. For, stepping beyond the boundaries of conventions, cultures, and religions, there are no social, moral, economic or political controls that normally keep a society relatively stable. The residents of Auroville, who are all volunteers, do not have a commonality of culture, language or education to hold them together, only the ideals of Auroville as specified in its Charter.

---

55 Collected Works of the Mother. Vol. 13: 229.
56 ibid.: 229.
57 ibid.: 229.
58 ibid.: 229.

The construction of Matrimandir has been an enormous project that has continued almost through the entire history of the township, and the design of its gardens and lake will continue for years to come. The building itself is completely symbolic, yet it is designed to functionally operationalize the values those symbols represent.

The Matrimandir houses an inner chamber for silent concentration, where a concentrated shaft of sunlight strikes a crystal of pure optical-quality glass. Surrounding this inner chamber and part of Matrimandir are twelve meditation chambers each designed to convey a specific quality of our human existence that is necessary for our spiritual growth. Radiating outwards from the Matrimandir, are twelve gardens that are part of this central area of peace. In accordance with the Mother's wishes, each of the twelve gardens of Matrimandir are being designed to express a particular power of the human being.

A unique feature for a city: The International Zone

Radiating outwards from the central peace area are the four zones of this city: the Cultural, Residential, Industrial and International Zones. While the first three zones are necessary elements of any human settlement, the International Zone is a singular and symbolic addition to Auroville as "a city of human unity." Sri Aurobindo's ideal of human unity is represented in Auroville not only by the diversity of its residents, who currently come from over fifty different countries, but also by this International Zone.

In the International Zone, all nations have been invited to establish a pavilion expressive of their national and cultural tradition. The Mother said, "The most important idea is that the unity of the human race can be achieved neither by uniformity nor by domination and subjection. Only a synthetic organization of all nations, each one occupying its true place according to its own genius and the part it has to play in the whole, can bring about a

comprehensive unification which has any chance of enduring."[59]
The International Zone represents a mini world-union, a learning
campus to experience the genius of every culture.

In his political writings, Sri Aurobindo posits that, like the
individual, each nation has a specific role to play in the world and
a soul that it seeks to manifest. The pavilions of the International
Zone, by presenting the living and vibrant exhibits of their
respective cultures, would be an embodiment of their respective
nation-souls. The Mother wished for nations to actively
participate in the building of the International Zone, stating that
such conscious collaboration will act "against the catastrophic
consequences of the error of armament."[60]

Governance: The Ideal of "Divine Anarchy"

*Organization is a discipline of action, but for Auroville
we aspire to go beyond organizations, which are
arbitrary and artificial. We want an organization that is
the expression of a higher consciousness working for the
manifestation of the truth of the future.*

The Mother

In order to allow the divine force to freely express itself
in the manifestation of Auroville, the Mother was always
extremely reluctant to give a definitive shape to Auroville's
governing organizations. She sought "to replace the mental
government of intelligence by the government of a spiritualized
consciousness",[61] stating that "it is the highest consciousness that
sees the most clearly – the most clearly and the most truly – what

---

59 Collected Works of the Mother. Vol. 13: 12.
60 Mother's Agenda. Vol. 9: 212.
61 ibid. Vol. 8: 454.

the needs of the most material thing should be."[62] The mental consciousness is radically different from that of a spiritual or a supramental consciousness. The mind formulates and organizes things to the best of its capability, but, as the Mother explains, the formulations of the mind tend to get fossilized and outdated. A spiritual consciousness, on the other hand, is flexible and progressively adapts itself to changing needs. In the early years of Auroville, the Mother specifically stated:

No rules or laws are being framed. Things will get formulated as the underlying truth of the township emerges and takes shape progressively.[63]

Terming the ideal political organization of Auroville "divine anarchy," the Mother explains that "the anarchic state is the self-government of each individual, and it will be the perfect government only when each one becomes conscious of the inner Divine and will obey only him and him alone."[64] The inner divine to which the Mother refers is the psychic being, the power of the soul evolving itself, and, when people are conscious of it, they can "organize themselves spontaneously, without fixed rules and laws."[65] Such an ideal organization, where people are conscious of their psychic beings and live according to the supramental truth, would automatically lead to a natural hierarchical harmony where everyone would find their place. It would result in an integral unity where individuality and diversity are not suppressed. The Mother time and again expressed her faith in the spiritual consciousness to work out things in its own way. She envisaged a small group with "intuitive intelligence" (people with "an intuition that

---

62 Mother's Agenda.Vol. 9: 108.
63 ibid. Vol. 8: 450.
64 ibid. Vol. 11: 76.
65 Collected Works of the Mother. Vol. 13: 224.

manifests intellectually")[66] governing Auroville. She spoke of a "hierarchic organization grouped around the most enlightened centre and submitting itself to a collective discipline".[67] In a text entitled "A Dream" she further explained:

In the general organization intellectual, moral and spiritual superiority will find expression not in the enhancement of the pleasures and the powers of life but in the increase of duties and responsibilities.[68]

Governance: The Current Reality

The present-day reality of Auroville appears quite different from the spiritual organization called for by the Mother, with none of the Aurovilians apparently having this greater spiritual authority. Since 1988, by an Act of the Indian Parliament, Auroville has the legal status of a Foundation. There was a contest for the legal ownership and management of Auroville after the Mother passed away in 1973. The matter was finally settled with the Indian Parliament recognizing that nobody could claim proprietary rights over Auroville as its Charter declared that it "belongs to humanity."

The Auroville Foundation came into being to ensure that the ideals of the Auroville Charter are the guiding principles for its realization. The Auroville Foundation is a three-tier organization comprising the Residents' Assembly of Auroville (consisting of Aurovilians above the age of eighteen), an International Advisory Council and a Governing Board. The Governing Board of the Auroville Foundation liaises with the Residents' Assembly of Auroville through the latter's selected body, the Working Committee.

---

66   Mother's Agenda. Vol. 9: 101.
67   Collected Works of the Mother. Vol. 13: 204.
68   ibid. Vol. 12: 94.

For all practical purposes, the Residents' Assembly is given full freedom to organize its governance in any way it chooses and, at present, Auroville is governed by a number of key working groups that have been identified and chosen through a participatory process by the community.

The working groups, such as the Entry Service, the Housing Board, the Budget Coordination Committee, the Human Resources team, the Working Committee, the Auroville Council, L'avenir d'Auroville, the Town Development Council and the Funds and Assets Management Committee, are mostly peer-based in their organizational structure. But without any effective hierarchy, internal group processes are often experienced as being interminably slow. Paradoxically, there is a hierarchy among the working groups, with the Working Committee, the Funds and Assets Management Committee, being apex bodies that often have the final say over many issues.

In the absence of laws, governance is based on increasing sets of guidelines and policies that have been adopted by the community. Governance, however, depends on the goodwill and cooperation of the residents, for there are practically no collective structures to enforce decisions. Decision-making often is a lengthy and cumbersome process as different view points are sought to be included through a process of consensus. If consensus cannot be achieved, a vote by the majority is used as a decision-making process. The challenges of a small community where the governed and those in governance often know one another personally is manifold. Other challenges include lack of full-time competent people available for serving in governing positions, insufficient institutional mechanisms to ensure that there is a continuity in each governing group, and increasing numbers of checks and balances in the system in an effort to ensure all the residents abide by the basic principles of Auroville. Admittedly, it is quite a challenge to govern an ever-growing and changing community, which also includes differences in cultural understanding and economic privileges. The residents of Auroville periodically experiment with different forms of organization in an attempt to manifest more closely the vision of the Mother with respect to the ideals of Auroville. But, as of today, it is felt that the anarchic spirit that was manifest in the early years of Auroville is missing. This, however, is in keeping with evolution of human societies throughout the ages, where one finds that as a society grows there is an increasing division of labour accompanied by an increasing complexity of governing policies and institutions.

The Ideal Economy

> *The aim of its [that of a spiritual society] economics would be not to create a huge engine of production, whether of the competitive or the co-operative kind, but to give to men – not only to some but to all men each in his highest possible measure – the joy of work according to their own nature, and free leisure to grow inwardly, as well as a simply rich and beautiful life for all.*
>
> Sri Aurobindo

In the spiritual society envisioned by Sri Aurobindo and the Mother, economics—the means of production of wealth and its distribution—is also viewed in terms of spiritual values rather than of material necessities. Foreseeing the eventual demise of both communism and capitalism, they stated that money was a power of the Divine. Individuals in possession of wealth were to ideally regard themselves as custodians entrusted with the task of using money for divine purposes. The Mother emphasized that both inheritance rights and accrual of interest on capital was not the way it was meant to be. She asserted that "money is not meant to make money. ... Money is meant to prepare the earth to manifest the new creation."[69] In "A Dream" the Mother elaborates on the ideal economy:

> *In this ideal place money would no longer be the sovereign lord; individual worth would have a far greater importance than that of material wealth and social standing. There, work would not be a way to earn one's living but a way to express oneself and to develop one's capacities and possibilities while being of service to the community as a whole, which, for its own part, would provide for each individual's subsistence and sphere of action. In short, it would be a place where human relationships, which are normally based almost exclusively on competition and strife, would be replaced by relationships of emulation in doing well, of collaboration and real brotherhood.[70]*

For Auroville, the Mother desired that money be a medium of exchange only with the outside world. Within Auroville, instead of monetary exchanges she wished to have a flexible system in which residents would not be taxed but voluntarily "contribute to the collective welfare in work, kind or money"[71] while they, in turn, would have their basic needs met by the community. The Mother distinguished between basic needs and desires, explaining that a spiritual seeker should not act from his ego and its desires, and that material needs decrease with the growth of the spiritual consciousness. From the very beginning, the Mother set up a collective distribution system, similar to the one she had established earlier in the Ashram, that distributed basic necessities to the Aurovilians.

---

69   Mother's Agenda. Vol. 10: 331.
70   ibid. Vol. 8: 450.
71   Collected Works of the Mother. Vol. 12: 94.

The Mother also specified that all Aurovilians work five hours daily for the common good. Ideally, work in Auroville is done in the spirit of Karma Yoga, that is, as an offering to the Divine. To the extent possible, the Mother emphasized the importance of Karma Yoga in Auroville, as it is only by a conscious engagement with the material world that one can transform it.

Auroville's shared economy is a far cry from mainstream commercialized society that seeks to monetize all transactions. Outside in mainstream society, based on capitalistic and patriarchic assumptions, some forms of works, such as domestic services, are grossly underpaid, while information technology services are well paid. In Auroville, all forms of work are sought to be equally valued. In the five decades of its existence, Auroville has experimented and continues to experiment with a number of different economic models. It encourages both individual enterprise and sharing. Commercial units are enjoined to contribute one-third of their profits to a common fund. The common fund partially or fully supports many basic community services, including education. And yet, the situation is far from ideal. For instance, despite Mother's injunctions to the contrary, there are almost triple the number of paid employees in Auroville than residents. And, as Auroville is not yet the self-supporting township the Mother hoped it to be, its economic base is inextricably linked to the regional, national and global economy.

Unending Education

> *In this place, children would be able to grow and develop integrally without losing contact with their souls; education would be given ... to enrich existing faculties and bring forth new ones.*
>
> *The Mother*

Auroville's Charter proclaims it to be a place of "unending education". As such, life in Auroville is a constant learning experience for the young and old alike. The Mother did not believe in formal educational systems geared towards passing examinations and getting certificates. As in the school that she started in the Ashram, for Auroville she wanted a "free progress" educational system, which she defined as "a progress guided by the soul and not subjected to habits, conventions or preconceived ideas."[72] The rationale behind such an educational system stems from the belief that "nothing can be taught to the mind which is not already concealed as potential knowledge in the unfolding soul of the creature."[73] Hoping to bring up children who would develop and sustain a conscious contact with their souls, the Mother allowed the students of the Ashram school immense freedom in choosing their curriculum. Advising the teachers of the Ashram school, the Mother said "One must help the student to become, as much as possible, what he can and wants to be – for if his soul has more or less chosen his life's destiny, yet what he shall make out of it is in no way determined. The child is not only a mind to be trained, but a consciousness that must be helped to grow and widen itself."[74]

An integral education, which fosters the physical, vital, mental, psychic (spiritual) development of the human personality, is offered to the students of the Ashram school. And while freedom is given to the students in choosing the subjects of their study, discipline in following their chosen subjects is insisted upon. Rather than emphasizing acquired mental knowledge, the focus is on perfecting the body, refining the senses through the arts, developing the will and training the mind for greater concentration.

---

72 Collected Works of the Mother: 170.
73 The Synthesis of Yoga: 54.
74 Collected Works of the Mother. Vol. 12: 117.

These principles of education that the Mother established for the Ashram school have served as general guidelines in Auroville. Mother gave names for the first schools in Auroville, which reflect her approach to education: Last School, After School, Super School, and No School. In its chequered history, education in Auroville has seen various forms, from the complete banning of schools to formal and non-formal systems, including home-schooling. Today, while most schools in Auroville tend to have a formalized approach with established classes or grades, there is flexibility within the system and individual attention is given to each student. In addition to crèches and kindergartens, one primary school is known as Transition School while there are two secondary schools: Last School and Future School. A University of Human Unity is still in the beginning stages of development. Apart from formal education, a plethora of classes, programmes, and workshops of all sorts are offered by various institutions of Auroville to cater to the learning needs of adults. Of all these institutions, Savitri Bhavan offers regular classes on Integral Yoga.

Auroville as an Experiment

Auroville is an experiment in collective realization.

The Mother

The Mother often refers to Auroville in transcendental terms, stating that the founding of this city was a divine decree and that the city already exists on an occult plane. She speaks of the divine force that especially aids Auroville by exerting a continual pressure on its citizens and she asserts that the ideal Auroville, even if it takes hundreds or even a thousand years, will one day be manifested on Earth. In one recorded conversation, she completely dismisses human agency, saying "it [the city] will be built by what is invisible to you. The men who have to act as instruments will do so despite themselves. They are only puppets in the hands of larger forces. Nothing depends on human beings – neither the planning nor the execution – nothing!"[75] Elsewhere, however, she admits that "in the details of the execution the human consciousness intervenes."[76] Perhaps above all, one has to bear in mind that, in numerous conversations, the Mother speaks of Auroville as an experiment that may act as a catalyst to hasten the earthly evolution from mind to Supermind.

It is a matter of conjecture as to how far the present-day reality of Auroville embodies Sri Aurobindo's and the Mother's far-reaching vision of human unity and world transformation. If we were to accept a transpersonal view of reality, it would be impossible for our limited rational minds to determine the veracity of Sri Aurobindo's vision or to gauge how far Auroville manifests that vision. On the one hand, Auroville, with its amazing diversity, is the largest and indeed the only experiment of its kind in the world. On the other hand, certain developments in present-day Auroville tend to contradict Mother's vision. For instance, aspects of the presence of the Indian Government via The Auroville Foundation, and Auroville's overwhelming dependence on a 5,000-strong hired labour force are not in keeping with the Mother's ideals. The city has also become a tourist destination for more than 90,000 per year. In the salubrious winter months, almost one-third of the people staying in Auroville are visitors. Such developments may be considered as problematic since the Mother's explicitly warns against Auroville having too much contact with the outside world. She speaks of the immense need for a divine protection to keep "infiltration or admixture" at bay and prevent the "nucleus [of the city] from falling back into an inferior creation."[77]

---

75 The Mother on Auroville: 13.
76 Collected Works of the Mother. Vol. 12: 248.
77 Mother's Agenda. Vol. 2: 270.

Paper Butterflies at the Youth Center, Auroville

In this context, one should bear in mind that both Sri Aurobindo and the Mother repeatedly said that the supramental force works out things in its own manner in ways that they could not entirely predict. Conditions on earth have definitely changed since the inception of Auroville. The past five decades have witnessed the end of the Cold War, the rise of the emerging economies. And the inexorable forces of globalizing capitalism and information technologies are reshaping the world at an unprecedented pace. Perhaps most importantly, ongoing planetary events – namely climate change and the developing sixth mass extinction – have brought to question the meaning of the whole human endeavour.

With such earth-shaping forces at work, one may well ask what can a little community, an eclectic international town in south India, contribute to human development and evolution?

The vision of Auroville and its dynamic spirit continues to attract people, but one may ask if the present-day reality of Auroville actually represents a unique evolutionary edge. For in some ways, Auroville seems to be behind the curve in innovation as one witnesses new forms of expression, new forms of working and of organization emerging all over the world. Aurovilians are keenly aware of the hiatus between the vision and the reality. In an effort towards bridging this gap, they continuously experiment with different collective structures. Most of them simultaneously engage in an inner spiritual quest in the belief that the inner consciousness shapes the outer manifestation of the city. Perhaps this is where the challenge and the promise of Auroville lies: the city is built from within.

Given the Mother's statement that it could take as long as a thousand years for the manifestation of an ideal Auroville, it is perhaps too early to gauge the success of Auroville in terms of its evolutionary impetus after just fifty years. Besides, Auroville's development is interlinked with the evolutionary momentum of the planet. As Sri Aurobindo states:

***With the present morality of the human race a sound and durable human unity is not yet possible; but there is no reason why a temporary approximation to it should not be the reward of strenuous aspiration and untiring effort. By constant approximations and by partial realizations and temporary successes, Nature advances.**[78]*

Such words encourage Aurovilians to persevere in this experiment in human unity in spite of all the inner and outer challenges that they face. For many Aurovilians, Integral Yoga gives meaning to their human endeavor, casting personal and collective life in a new and purposeful perspective. And in turn, the living reality of Auroville continues to inspire many individuals and groups all over the world.

---

78   Essays Divine and Human: 467.

International Publications

Auroville Architecture
by Franz Fassbender

Auroville Form Style and Design
by Franz Fassbender

Landscapes and Gardens of Auroville
by Franz Fassbender

Inauguration of Auroville
by Franz Fassbender

Auroville in a Nutshell
by Tim Wrey

Death doesn't exist
The Mother on Death, Sri Aurobindo on Rebirth
Compiled by Franz Fassbender

Divine Love
Compiled by Franz Fassbender

Five Dream
by Sri Aurobindo

A Vision
Compiled by Franz Fassbender

Passage to More than India
by Dick Batstone

The Mother on Japan
Compiled by Franz Fassbender

Children of Change: A Spiritual Pilgrimage
by Amrit (Howard Shoji Iriyama)

Memories of Auroville - told by early Aurovilians
by Janet Feran

Featured Titles

Divine Love

The texts presented in this book are selected from the Mother and Sri Aurobindo.
"Awakened to the meaning of my heart. That to feel love and oneness is to live. And this the magic of our golden change, is all the truth I know or seek, O sage."

Sri Aurobindo, Savitri, Book XII, Epilog

A Vision by the Mother

On 28th May 1958, the Mother recounted a vision she once had of a wonderful Being of Love and Consciousness, emanated from the Supreme Origin and projected directly into the Inconscient so that the creation would gradually awaken to the Supramental Consciousness. The Mother's account of this vision was brought out a first time in November 1906, in the Revue Cosmique, a monthly review published in Paris.

A Dream – Aims and Ideals of Auroville
the Mother on Auroville

50 years of Auroville from 28.02.1968 - 28.02.2018
Today, information about Auroville is abundant. Many people try to make meaning out of Auroville – about its conception, to what direction should we grow towards, and, what are we doing here?

But what was Mother's original Dream and what was her Vision for Auroville back then?

Matrimandir Talks by the Mother

This book presents most of Mother's Matrimandir talks, including how she conceived the idea for this special concentration and meditation building in Auroville.

Memories of Auroville - Told by early Aurovilians

Memories of Auroville is a book about the very early days of Auroville based on interviews made in 1997 with Aurovilians who lived here between 1968 and 1973. The interviews presented in this book are part of a history program for newcomers that I had created with my friend, Philip Melville in 1997. The plan was to divide Auroville's history into different eras and then interview Aurovilians according to their area of knowledge. Our first section would cover the years from 1968 till 1973 when the Mother was still in her physical body.

The Way of the Sunlit Path

May The Way of the Sunlit Path be a convenient guide for activating this ancient truth as a support for a Conscious Evolution.
May it illumine the transformation offered to us in the Integral Yoga.

A Dream Takes Shape (in English, French, Hindi)

A comprehensive brochure on the international township of Auroville in, ranging from its Charter and "Why Auroville?" to the plan of the township, the central Matrimandir, the national pavilions and residences, to working groups, the economy, making visits, how to join, its relationship to the Sri Aurobindo Ashram, and its key role in the future of the world. This brochure endeavours to highlight how The Mother envisioned Auroville from its inception, some of the major achievements realised over the years, and some of the difficulties currently faced in implementing the guidelines which she gave.

Mother on Japan

I had everything to learn in Japan. For four years, from an artistic point of view, I lived from wonder to wonder. And everything in this city, in this country, from beginning to end, gives you the impression of impermanence, of the unexpected, the exceptional... ...everything in this city, in this country, from beginning to end, gives you the impression of impermanence, of the unexpected, the exceptional. You always come to things you did not expect; you want to find them again and they are lost – they have made something else which is equally charming.

Auroville Reflected

On 28 February 1968, on an impoverished plateau on the Coromandel Coast of South India, about 4,000 people from around the world gathered for a most unusual inauguration. Handfuls of soil from the countries of the world were mixed together as a symbol of human unity. Why did Indira Gandhi, the erstwhile Prime Minister of India, support this development for "a city the earth needs?" Why did UNESCO endorse this project? Why does the Dalai Lama continue to be involved in the project? What led anthropologist Margaret Mead to insist that records must be kept of its progress? Why did both historian William Irwin Thompson and United Nations representative Robert Muller note that this social experiment may be a breakthrough for humanity even as critics commented, "it is an impossible dream"?

A House For the Third Millennium

Essays on Matrimandir

Nightwatch at the Matrimandir...
A cosmic spectacle; the black expanse above, the big black crater of Matrimandir's excavation carved deep into the soil. The four pillars - two of which are completed and the other two nearing completion - are four huge ships coming together from the four corners of the earth to meet at this pro propitious spot...

Passage to More than India

This book is a voyage of discovery. In 1959 the author, Dick Batstone, a classically educated bookseller in England, with a Christian background, comes across a life of the great Indian polymath Sri Aurobindo, though a series of apparently fortuitous circumstances. A meeting in Durham, England, leads him to a determination to get to the Sri Aurobindo Ashram in Pondicherry, a former French territory south of Madras.